To See My Own World

a collection of poems

Anamarie Davis-Wilkins

To See My Own World

Copyright © 2023 Anamarie Davis-Wilkins

All rights reserved.

ISBN: 979-8-218-33047-7

To See My Own World

DEDICATION

With my whole heart to:

My son, daughter, and grandchildren

and the rest of my family.

Also, for anyone who wished they said it, but didn't.

To See My Own World

CONTENTS

	Acknowledgments	i
1	In My Head	Pg 2
2	Pen to Paper	Pg 5
3	Changed My Name	Pg 7
4	Be Fed	Pg 10
5	All in the Walk	Pg 13
6	Who's Next	Pg 15
7	Innervoice	Pg 18
8	Open Mike	Pg 21
9	What's Next?	Pg 23
10	The Tree	Pg 26
11	A Time.	Pg 29
12	*4745*	Pg 33
13	Good Food Anxiety	Pg 35
14	A Tribute to Brown v Board	Pg 37
15	Cries	Pg 39
16	These Hands	Pg 41
17	Untitled 3	Pg 43
18	Inflation	Pg 45
19	The Whisper	Pg 47
20	Us	Pg 49

21	Untitled 1	Pg 51
22	Bounce	Pg 53
23	Bastard Narrative	Pg 55
24	Untitled 2	Pg 58
25	Word Jar	Pg 60
26	Sing that Blues Man	Pg 62
27	IKU	Pg 65
28	Random	Pg 67
29	She Writes	Pg 69
30	Rain Gang	Pg 71
31	Honey!	Pg 73
32	White Gaze	Pg 75
33	*Black Caviar' *	Pg 77
	About the Author	Pg 78

ACKNOWLEDGMENTS

To My Most High, for giving me the words and voice. A whole hearted thank you and the biggest hug I can muster, to T.L. and Tyla. It took your support and encouragement to make me follow this through. You were my extra pair of eyes and ears and sounding board. Thank you again, for helping make yet another dream come true.

To See My Own World

Like many people, I sometimes suffer from fleeting thoughts that keep me awake or unable to concentrate.

This poem is a technique I used, to calm

those thoughts. I do not promote

the use of alcohol nor CBD/THC

To See My Own World

In My Head

The heaviest burdens

that we carry are the thoughts

in our head.

These thoughts that are

leaping, jumping, running

and racing.

Rage, screams, regrets, worry

and terror, rapidly flooding

the space where

Peace, calmness, and contentment

should be instead.

Edible gummies, a glass of wine,

smooth jazz playing

to take me where peace lives.

Floating on the notes of blue to gold,

like a streak of lightning

that sends shivers down my spine.

Swaying, rocking, humming, fingers snapping,

and foot tapping, goodness that spread.

Taking a deep breath to exhale

and letting go of the

burdens of the thoughts

that was in my head.

To See My Own World

To See My Own World

Pen to Paper

A writer is like

an artist.

Painting the universe

with words, stories, pictures,

plots, stanzas, and proses.

A trade where we stand alone.

We allow the world to hope, dream, imagine

think and heal.

The power of pen to paper shone.

To See My Own World

This poem almost speaks for itself.

It came from an encounter I had with a young man, whom I once babysat.

It also reflects how disrespectful

some teens/young adults can be.

Changed My Name

I told Jesus

it would be alright

If HE changed my name.

I said, Jesus,

not you boy,

who I once changed diapers

and now you call yourself and man, and hence,

you decide to change my name.

The insaneness, the craziness,

let me give you a few pennies

to buy yourself some sense.

Did you think about your mother?

The she in your family and the ancestors of her.

Foul words spewing out your mouth,

in a disrespectful, immature blur.

You changed my name

to bitch and hoe, just to name a few,

if you looked in the mirror,

you would see that the names you called me, are the names I changed yours too.

Now change my name to what it is supposed to be, Miss, Maim,

woman, lady, Mzee, Jameela

Then and only then, it will be alright if YOU

                      changed my name.

To See My Own World

This is simply about facing

your own truth. And being open-minded

to being a better you to enjoy life.

To See My Own World

Be Fed.

Full,

not bellies

but spirit and mind.

Open mind

like open mouths

to face the truth

Even if it's unkind.

Bold steps outside the box,

stepping in it

around it and through it.

Believe it or not

people are looking at you,

don't be afraid, just do it.

Crazy,

lost of mind,

because you seek happiness of all kinds.

Fierce out loud,

dreams to shine brighter,

be a stepping stone for others.

Filled up on laughter, fairness and happiness.

Filled up with life and love of all kind.

Full.

All in the Walk

As I walk, it is with

confidence, pride, and control.

As I walk, it is with

my whole being of creativity

and sensibility.

As I walk, it is only

women like myself

who knows the struggles

in the footsteps I leave behind.

As I walk, it is with

the attitude and toughness, that

I have adorned because

of past inequalities.

As I walk, it is with

wit and courage

that will take me

a step closer to victory.

This one speaks to how,

We are still fighting racism.

It poses the question of who, if anyone,

will become our next Champion.

Who's Next!

From you to me,

can you see

what I see,

hatred and evil all around me.

Poor children

Poor broke

Poor old

Everyone trying to get their own gold.

My heart cries

like a mother to all

wounded and bewildered

as I watch society fall.

We pray, we hope,

we hope, we pray,

that if we wake up tomorrow,

it will be a different kind of day.

Malcolm

Martin

To See My Own World

Gandhi

Pope John

Single moms raising good kids and training

them not to be a con.

The race was run,

generations gone to waste

which soldiers are going

to take their place.

Innervoice

It was the small innervoice

of a young black girl, big-eyed, innocent, and shy.

Wondering, hoping, trying to understand,

the separation of two races and why.

Whites only, coloreds stand behind the line,

dizzying spew of words, from those that

didn't recognize, she too, was of mankind.

Innervoice screaming, red with anger,

white with hatred and blue from holding her words.

Now a wide eyed, found voice, mature woman,

knowing but still trying to understand,

the separation of all races,

whites to blues, constant attacks, with Karens

all up in our faces.

Innervoice screaming,

Not Again! No More! No More!

Mature woman speaks boldly

for the ancestor that couldn't,

and for those who spoke and died

when society thought they shouldn't.

To See My Own World

Open Mike

Spoken, written, inner voice

speaking meaningful, powerful elements

that are of that singular language.

Making remarks that give

accounts with the assurance

of a promise of that distinct action.

A verbal signal to speak of

and write about.

Words!

What is this?

What is this,

that you think defines me?

When was the punishment imposed

for the laws that were not broken.

When did the infringement of rules,

charges, sanctions, and penance

fall upon me.

Was it on that 6th day of the first week in Genesis?

What is that,

that you think defines me? What defines you?

For your history is my history,

so mingled together,

yet we withstand all the misery.

Name taken

Genealogy hidden

To See My Own World

Genius/ Riches stolen

Language silenced

Customs copied

History not mentioned

What was, and what is

this strange penalty

for being born black?

The Tree

Ripe fruit still hangs

on the old ancestral tree,

thick trunk with roots so deeply buried,

they will never pull free.

Branches twist

and reach for nowhere but everywhere,

clutching to the memory fruit

once there.

Wild winds blow,

as natures nutrients

ensures this tree will grow.

Thunder moves the ground

lightning lights the sky.

Spirits of my ancestors dance in the rain

while praising the heavens up high.

Morning comes

ancestral tree still proudly holds its crown,

while strange fruit has fallen out,

spotting the muddy ground.

To See My Own World

I was listening to 70's music,

and images flooded my mind.

This poem speaks of that era and some

events that I experienced.

A Time!

Do you remember that day?

I mean are you hip too when

people stood shoulder to shoulder,

everyone was accepted

and ignored color.

It was power to the people!

Right on! Right on!

Jimi Hendrix, psychedelic, supersonic funk,

with hippie flowers,

black power

The revolution will be televised.

Yet, there was peace, love

Shots fired, beatdowns

fists up, gobs of spit

cracked skulls, fires blazing,

burning tears that make you choke,

riots in the streets

hope gone up in smoke.

Marvin Gaye's "What's Going On ', blaring,

Stop the war! No to Vietnam shouts, Maryjane, and psychotropics

all that didn't stop the brotherly love,

but it was not the love that Dr. King spoke about.

That was years of time

and time this time,

it's guns, crack and crank to get lit,

zombies frozen in place,

emaciated bodies,

blank eyes stares and senseless crimes

just to buy the next hit.

What happened melting pot?

Yes, it was the 'Me Decade"

it was decided that,

it was time to escape and look inward

to find oneself.

It was a place in time, when we were here nor there

but everywhere.

Were we disillusioned with the strikes,

the wishes, and the want.

Are we living that continuing circle of time,

and it's still all about "me".

For today it takes

tragedy and catastrophe,

before we stand

shoulder to shoulder,

everyone is accepted,

color ignored

and then, it becomes "We".

To See My Own World

This poem pains me even today.

He was a family member, 13 years old. A friend playing with a gun ended his life.

4745

4745 days

I said, 4745 days

That's all we had.

A bullet crashed into his head,

an open mouth, screamed from deep in the soul.

    From the pain far beyond the physical body,

    For both, a breath never returned.

Happy Thanksgiving!

Good Food Anxiety

The smell of that turkey in the oven

kept me up that night.

My mind thinking about the

snapping of beans,

shucking of corn,

mashing potatoes,

kneading of bread,

fluting of pies and

Lord, there better not be a lump in the gravy.

All hands on deck,

for the pot stirring,

sample tasting and ensuring enough

for the masses.

I finally drift off to sleep,

thankful for the bounty of my family

and the harvest of the meal to come.

A tribute to Brown vs. Board of Education 70th Anniversary (2023)

Education of whites.

Miseducation of blacks.

New books in hands,

that would never be in rotation,

even kept us from us,

just because of location.

Kept us separated,

Segregated.

It took a lawsuit for us

to be integrated,

Justice was not blind,

her scales tipped in favor

of the plaintiff for victory,

the whole world learned

when Brown vs. Board made history.

To See My Own World

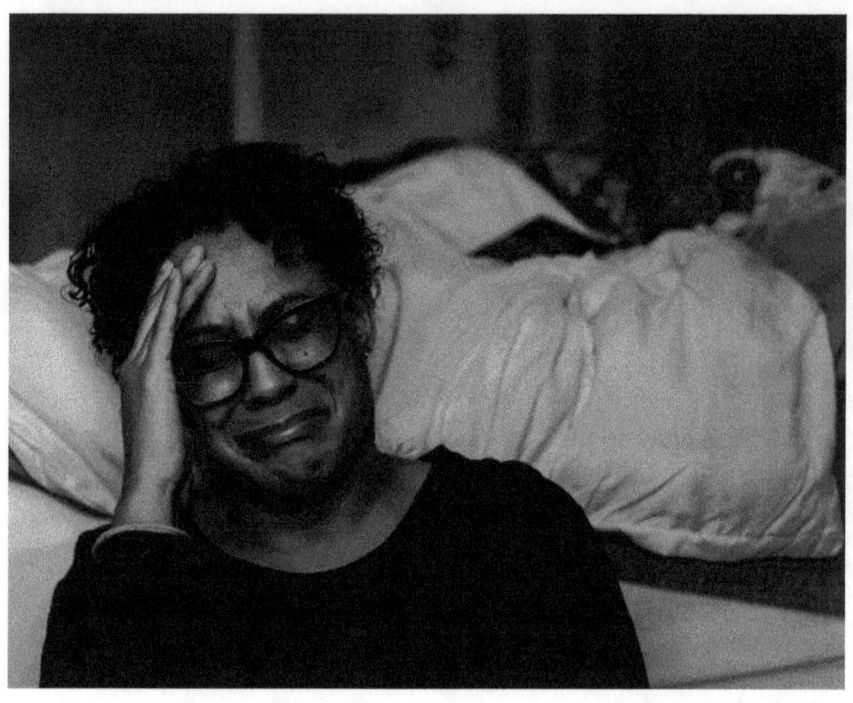

Israel- Hamas War (Gaza) and 9 other countries, and the crimes of recent in Topeka, Kansas 10/2023

Cries

I hear your cries,

mothers of the world.

Cries from the pain of war

and senseless acts of crimes.

We have cried enough

to fill every bank of

every river and ocean.

Scream my sisters.

Scream until you

shake the heavens,

so that it makes room

for our stars.

Pray my sisters.

That the darkness of evil

Dissipates like the dew

in the early morning.

And the rays of goodness and hope

shine like the mid-day sun.

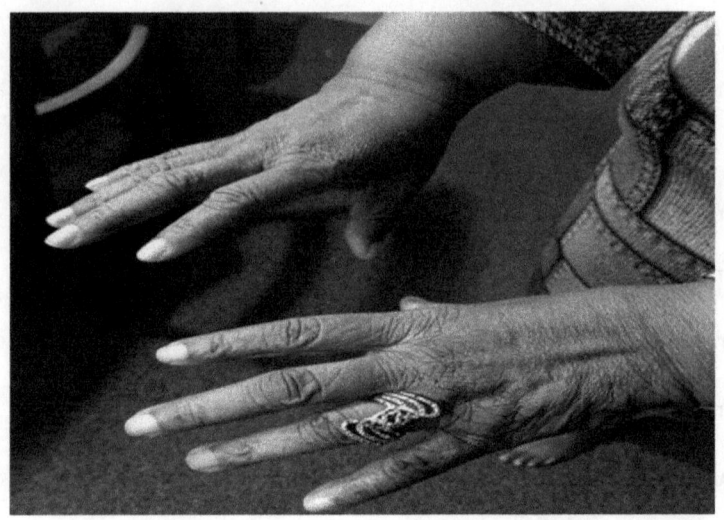

These Hands

These hands

are the hands,

that hands a mom

her new born baby.

Hands that are aged, and calloused, yet

gentle and strong.

These hands,

 help future, bring itself

into the present.

These hands,

gently swaddle future,

in a cloth hug

and I whisper, hello.

To See My Own World

Untitled 3

The seasons change

like the color of autumn leaves.

Summer heat and sweat

goes away

for the cool autumn breeze.

Everything is expensive nowadays!

Inflation

If I had a dime,

for every time,

and every time,

I had a dime,

It was gone.

To See My Own World

Just A Funny!!!

The Whisper

You turned to me,

leaned in and your

soft breath caressed my ear.

You spoke words,

with passion in your eyes.

I leaned into you,

my lips brushing

your cheek to ear.

      What?

Us

I came without

excuse and pretense,

hoping and waiting

for our evolution together.

    It never happened.

To See My Own World

This poem came to me in a dream.

I interpreted it as escaping my past, where I seemed lost.

And finding myself.

Untitled 1

I ran in the direction

of the sun.

Heart racing,

fast feet moving,

escaping the darkness behind me.

My mind racing with me,

it too taking

the jarring leaps of the

explained, unexplained

complicated reasons.

I took flight that day,

fleeing across space and time,

only to suddenly slam,

into a mirrored image of myself,

and I landed on me.

To See My Own World

NOT TWERKING!!!

Bounce

Her buttocks bounced,

in the flowing skirt.

But it was the wind

that blew it up,

   Ahh.. red panties.

This came from the observation

of my friend's relationship.

the things some women do,

to stay in a with a man.

The Bastard Narrative

In the beginning,

he told her he loved her.

whispered sweet whatnots

saying she was perfect, Then

                        She was not it. Something was wrong with her.

He told her he loved her but,

She had to change her hair.

She had to change her breasts.

She had to change her body.

She had to change her face.

                        She was not it. Something was wrong with her.

He told her he loved her but,

She had to change the way she cooked.

She had to change the way she ate.

She had to change the way she dressed.

She had to change the way she spoke.

> She was not it. Something was wrong with her.

He told her he loved her,

but his narrative was

of a secret agenda.

She said she loved him too, but

she changed her mind.

> He was not it. Something was wrong with him.

To See My Own World

Untitled 2

I gave up my ghost,

allowing it to leave

in broad daylight,

instead of under the cover of darkness.

Giving it up,

left me with a strange feeling

of euphoria, sudden contentment, and freedom.

I watched it

make shadows on the sidewalk,

Moving and shape-shifting into inanimate objects and finally

bind itself to an alley wall.

It sighed, when

I told it to,

"Stay there, until the next soul comes by".

A STANZA!!!

Word Jar

I used to seal

curse words in a jar.

One day, I forgot

to close the lid.

To See My Own World

Sing that blues man...

It was blues playing

in the old juke joint.

Smoke filled air

floating like a mystical mist,

circling, dragging, melancholy,

rich melodious tones

that echo like dominoes hitting the table.

This music with power,

to make you feel good or bad.

The notes and refrains, I was unaware of, were just as powerful

as the ones I knew.

Power that nudged you

to places, sometimes

if you submitted, it just happened.

People paused and listened

like a set on a stage

of mannequins instead of humans.

Stiff with pose and silent, as the music

was a confronting unreal confrontation.

This music knowing one's emotions and conflicts,

describes the drama and heartache of most black people's lives.

It escapes through windows and doors,

becoming a pedestrian.

crossing boundaries and going

to other parts of the world, without us looking.

IKU = Yoruba (debt keeper, death connection to the market)

Iku

Don't follow it into the darkness.

It will only penetrate

your body, turning your blood

into crystalized stones

that will flow like water,

Only bad angels

go to that church.

Kneeling to and prophesying

to its followers.

As they offer up souls

for material things.

Cultivated, selected

mortals of once godly beings,

with tantalizing visions

of success and grandeur.

Drained is the heart of compassion and mercy.

Forked tongues to sharp ears

molest the sense of righteousness and decency.

Manipulated dollars

for designer highs and consequential lows.

It will metamorph

into a thousand different entities

of glamourous, golden, shiny objects.

Don't follow it into the darkness.

You will forever be

a robotic, artificial intelligent, disassembled

form of your human self.

Random are the thoughts of a silent moment!

She Writes

There is a woman who

controls the pen. She writes

prose and haikus, but she smiles at the words

she tapped from flashes of memories,

like light bulbs of flower buds.

blooming is her poem.

To See My Own World

Rain Gang

Once a raindrop fell

on my head, which I hated.

It was wet and cold and called its friends

to gang me. I tried to shield by holding up my arms,

but their hits became more frequent. So, I stood

perfectly still and listened, to the

tap, drip, drops rhythms and I began to dance.

To See My Own World

Honey!

You are the rays,

that warm me

in the mornings.

The sugar,

 in my sweet tea in the afternoons.

The intoxication from my wine, in the evenings.

To See My Own World

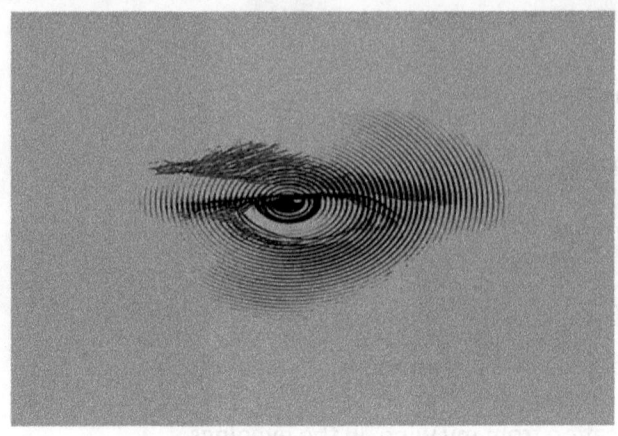

White Gaze

Minds were primed,

by the Constitution,

which gave them entitlement.

Those laws

and their history become their theology.

Our deaths are their contentment. So, they

look at us with hate, yet they want to be us, and they are

supposedly afraid of us.

Their stares are still

those of the mentally distorted

master psychological haze, known all too well as

the White Gaze.

To See My Own World

Black Caviar

Her tiny womb was the delicate housing

for the predetermined number of eggs,

she was born with.

Trauma from an unwelcomed, violent,

perpetrator's penetration destroyed it.

Stainless steel sliced through her flesh,

with steady hands. Hands that were supposed to heal.

But they belonged to a human without sympathy or empathy and overshadowed her humanity.

Cut out, sucked out, twisted tied, burnt ends.

reconfigured something that was not dead.

She was the rarest most expensive sturgeon,

robbed of her future babies.

Black Caviar (roe)

ABOUT THE AUTHOR

Anamarie Davis-Wilkins is a proud mom, grandmother, Birth Doula, writer, and poet, who lives in Topeka, Kansas. She has enjoyed reading and writing since childhood and continues to do so. Her first published books were a book of poetry, *Reminiscence,* and her first novel, *Under and Over.* She wrote and has had the play, If I Had a Sermon, performed at several venues. She has also a piece, Good Food Anxiety, published by the Poet Laureate of Kansas. She has had work published in numerous anthologies and online magazines. She is an active participant in Speak Easy Poets of Topeka, The Sunflower Poetry Society of Kansas, National Federation of State Poetry Societies and The Writers Guild.

www.ingramcontent.com/pod-product-compliance
Lightning Source LLC
Chambersburg PA
CBHW060415050426
42449CB00009B/1972